Science Alive

Magnets

Terry Jennings

A⁺

Smart Apple Media

Smart Apple Media is published by Black Rabbit Books
P.O. Box 3263, Mankato, Minnesota 56002

Printed in China

Created by Q2A Media
Editor: Honor Head
Senior Art Designers: Ashita Murgai, Nishant Mudgal
Designer: Harleen Mehta
Picture Researcher: Poloumi Ghosh
Line Artists: Indernil Ganguly, Rishi Bhardhwaj
Illustrators: Kusum Kala, Sanyogita Lal

Library of Congress Cataloging-in-Publication Data
Jennings, Terry J.
    Magnets / Terry Jennings.
    p. cm.—(Smart apple media. Science alive)
    Includes index.
    Summary: "Explains esssential facts about magnets, including magnetic fields, Earth's magnetism, electromagnets, and magnetic trains. Includes experiments"—Provided by publisher.
    ISBN 978-1-59920-272-3
    1. Magnets—Juvenile literature. 2. Magnetism—Juvenile literature. 3. Magnetic materials—Juvenile literature. 4. Magnetism—Experiments—Juvenile literature. I. Title.
QC757.5 J464 2009
538'.4—dc22
                                                                                    2007052819

All words in **bold** can be found in "Words to Remember" on pages 30–31.

Web site information is correct at time of going to press. However, the publishers cannot accept liability for any information or links found on third-party web sites.

9 8 7 6 5 4 3 2 1

Contents

Magnets

There are probably lots of magnets in your home. A few may be on your fridge door, but most are out of sight, inside machines and electronics.

What Is a Magnet?

A **magnet** is a piece of metal that **attracts,** or pulls, some materials towards it. Every magnet has two ends. These are called the magnet's north pole and south pole. The **poles** are the parts of a magnet where its forces, or magnetism, are strongest.

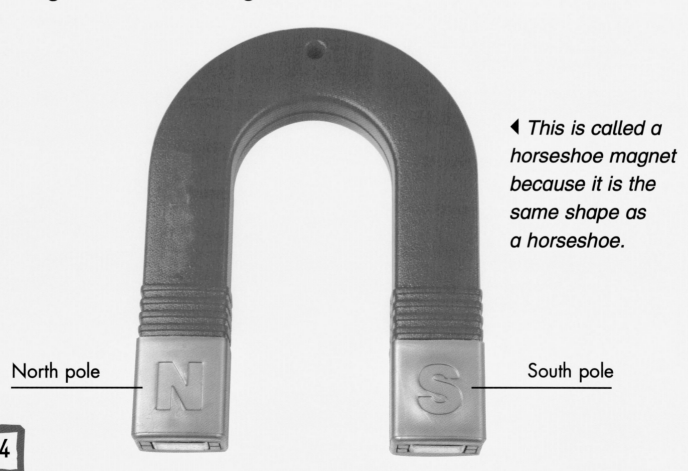

◀ *This is called a horseshoe magnet because it is the same shape as a horseshoe.*

North pole

South pole

Magnetic Force

Magnets make things move with an invisible force. This is called a magnetic force. Try pulling a wire paper clip off a magnet. Feel the magnetic force pulling back. You have to pull more strongly than the magnet to remove the paper clip.

▼ *You can see a magnetic force when you try to pull an object towards a magnet.*

Magnetic Metals

Only a few materials are attracted to a magnet. They are the metals iron, cobalt, and nickel. Most kinds of steel are also attracted to a magnet because they contain iron.

▲ *Forks and spoons are often made from stainless steel, which contains iron. The more iron they have, the more magnetic they will be.*

Magnetic Field

The space around a magnet where the invisible force of magnetism acts is called its **magnetic field.** Scientists draw lines to show how far a magnet's power stretches. Where the lines are close together, the magnetic force is greater than where the lines are spread out.

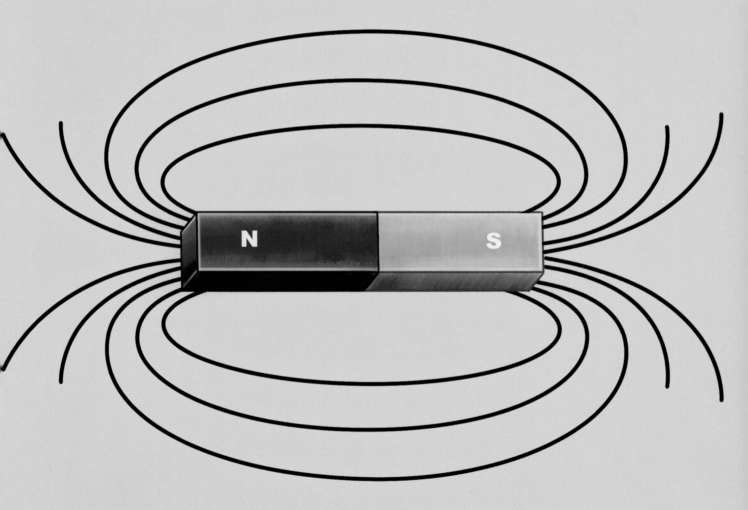

▲ *The magnetic force of a magnet is strongest at the north and south poles.*

Poles Apart

Magnets push and pull each other. If you put two north poles together, they push each other apart. We say they **repel** each other. Two south poles also repel each other. But if you put a north pole and a south pole together, they will attract each other.

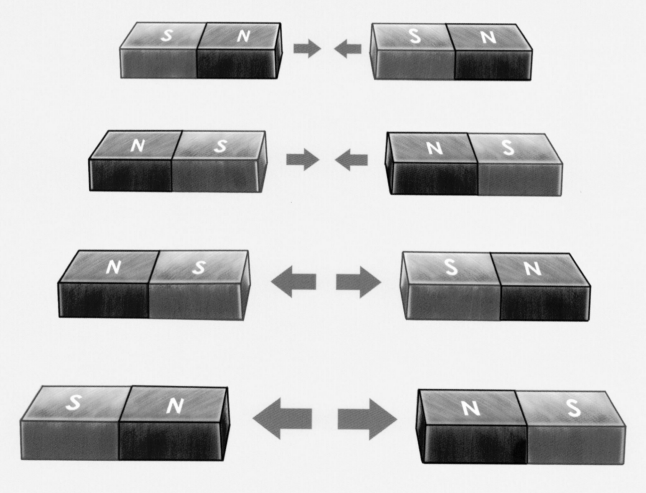

▲ *A north pole and a south pole attract each other. Two north poles or two south poles repel each other.*

Why Is It Magnetic?

Magnetic materials are made of millions of tiny magnetic pieces. The tiny magnetic pieces all face different directions, so they do not have any magnetic power. In a magnet, all the magnetic pieces face the same way, which is why it has magnetic power. Materials such as paper do not contain magnetic pieces so they are not magnetic.

▶ *Materials that are not attracted to magnets, such as these plastic and paper picnic things, are called non-magnetic.*

Try This...
Magnetic Fields

Find your magnet's magnetic field.

You Will Need
- a magnet • a sheet of stiff white paper or cardboard
- iron filings

1 Place the magnet on a level table.

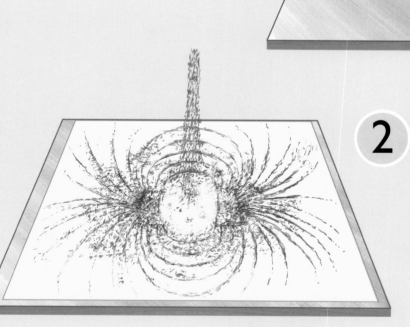

2 Put the sheet of paper or cardboard on top of the magnet. Sprinkle iron filings onto the paper or cardboard.

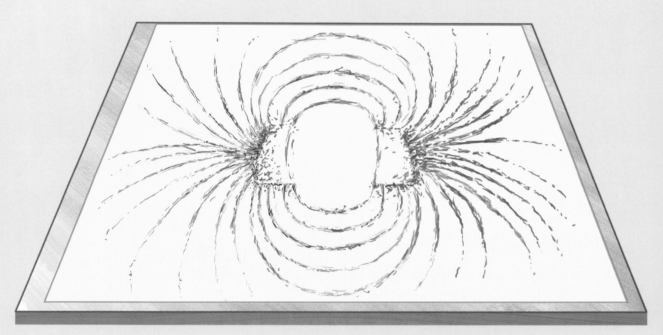

3 Gently tap the paper or cardboard. The iron filings form a pattern around the magnet. The pattern shows the magnetic field.

What happened?

The iron filings form curved lines that link the magnet's poles. These are the magnet's **lines of force**. Tapping the card helps to shake the iron filings into line. There are lots of iron filings at the magnet's poles, because that is where the magnetic force is the strongest.

Electromagnets

Magnets can also be made by using electricity. These magnets are called **electromagnets**. Their magnetism can be switched on and off.

Electricity and Magnets

If you put a piece of iron inside a coil of wire and pass an electric current through the wire, the iron becomes a strong electromagnet. If you switch off the electricity, the iron quickly loses most of its magnetism. This is how electromagnets work.

▶ *An electromagnetic crane will only pick up iron and steel when the electricity is switched on. The iron and steel drop back down when the electricity is switched off.*

Using Electromagnets

Powerful electromagnets are found in hospitals. They are used to remove iron or steel splinters from eyes. Electric bells, telephones, and the **loudspeakers** in radios, television sets, and music systems also use electromagnets.

▶ *There is a tiny electromagnet inside the earpiece of this telephone.*

Magnet Motors

Electric motors contain magnets that help to turn electricity into movement. Machines called **generators** use magnets to produce electricity.

Magnets and Coils

In a **power plant,** generators are used to produce electricity for our homes and streets. The generators are made of a huge magnet surrounded by a coil of copper wire. When the generator is turned, it produces electricity.

▶ *Wind turbines have a small generator in a box at the top of the pole. The generator is turned by the blades, which are turned by the wind.*

Electric Motors

Magnetic forces inside a motor, even a simple motor, change electricity into movement. In an **electric motor**, a coil of wire is placed between the poles of a horseshoe magnet. When electricity is sent through the wire, it makes the coil become magnetic.

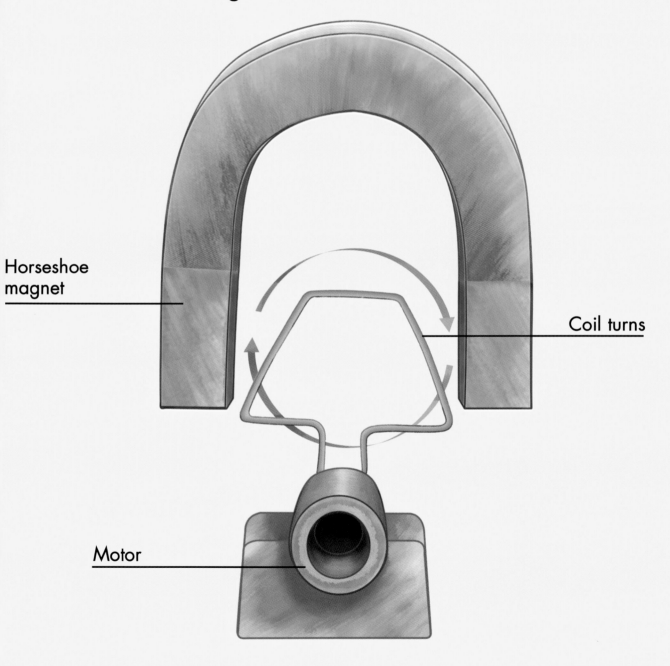

Horseshoe magnet

Coil turns

Motor

▲ *The horseshoe magnet makes the coil turn.*
As the coil spins around, it turns the motor.

Try This...
Find the Magnet

Hide and find your magnet.

You Will Need
• a selection of keys, paper clips, and other objects that stick to a magnet • a small magnet (perhaps a fridge magnet) • some envelopes
• a bar magnet

1 Seal each item inside an envelope including the small magnet, so you can't tell where the magnet is.

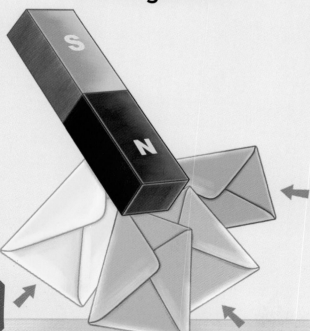

2 Bring one end of the bar magnet to the envelopes.

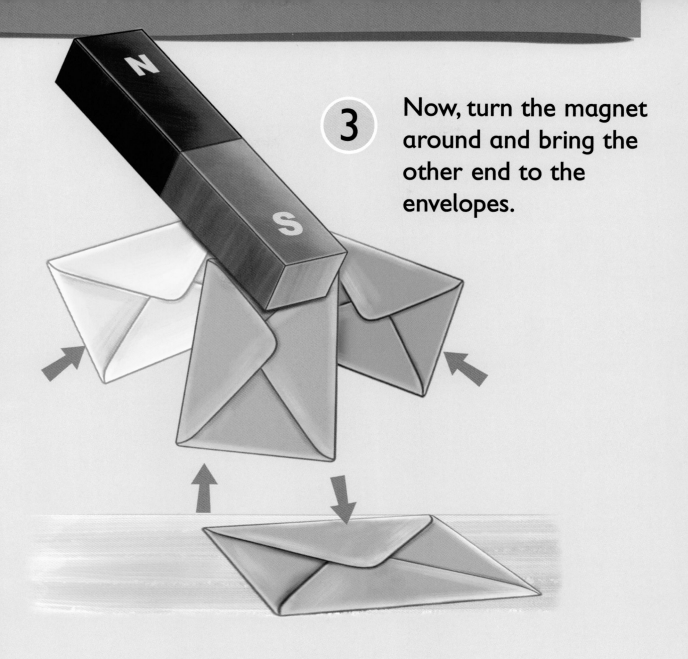

3 Now, turn the magnet around and bring the other end to the envelopes.

What happened?

Nearly all of the envelopes stick to the bar magnet's north pole and its south pole. But one envelope will stick to only one of the bar magnet's poles and not the other. This envelope contains the small magnet and it only sticks to one pole of the bar magnet, because opposite poles attract and like poles repel.

Earth's Magnetism

The whole planet Earth behaves like a giant bar magnet. It has a North Pole and a South Pole, just like a magnet. The Earth's magnetic field is all around us.

Compasses

Pilots, sailors, explorers, and other travelers use a **compass** to find their way. The needle of a compass is really a tiny magnet. Whichever way you hold the compass, the needle always swings around until it points north towards Earth's magnetic North Pole.

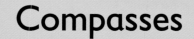

◀ *This boy uses a compass to make sure he is going in the right direction.*

Liquid Metal

Of course, there is not really a giant bar magnet inside the Earth. The Earth is magnetic because its **core** is made mainly of iron. Only the center of the core is solid. It is surrounded by liquid metal. As Earth spins, the liquid metal moves and produces the magnetic field.

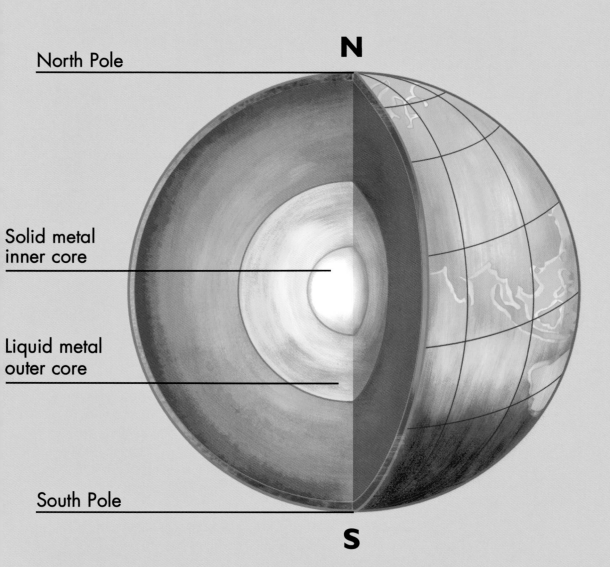

North Pole

N

Solid metal
inner core

Liquid metal
outer core

South Pole

S

Try This...
Power Magnets

Test the strength of different magnets.

You Will Need
• a selection of different magnets • a handful of paper clips

1 Hang a paper clip from one pole of one magnet.

2 Hang another paper clip from the end of the first one. Keep hanging paper clips until the magnet can hold no more.

3 Do the same with the other magnets. Count the number of paperclips.

What happened?

When the first paper clip is hung from the magnet, it becomes a tiny magnet. The next paper clip is magnetized, too, but not as strongly as the first. The last paper clip is magnetized so weakly that it cannot hold up another one. The strongest magnet is the one that holds the longest chain of paperclips.

Nature's Magnets

Many animals use the Earth's magnetic field to find their way on long journeys from one part of the world to another.

A Long Journey

Many birds, such as geese, go on long journeys across the world each year. They fly from the place where their young are born in the spring to a warmer place for the winter. Scientists believe the birds use the Earth's magnetic field to guide them across the world.

▲ *The long journeys made by many animals are called migrations.*

Turtle Maps

As soon as tiny loggerhead turtles hatch in the sand, they make their way to the sea. Once they are in the water, they swim thousands of miles to find food. Scientists think they find their way by sensing the Earth's magnetic field.

▲ *Scientists believe that loggerhead turtles are born with a magnetic map of the Atlantic Ocean in their brain.*

Try This...
Make a Compass

Use a sewing needle to make a compass.

You Will Need

• a steel needle • a bar magnet • a piece of cork or a piece of cardboard • a bowl of water

1 First you need to turn your needle into a magnet. Stroke the needle 20 times against the north pole of the bar magnet, always stroking in the same direction.

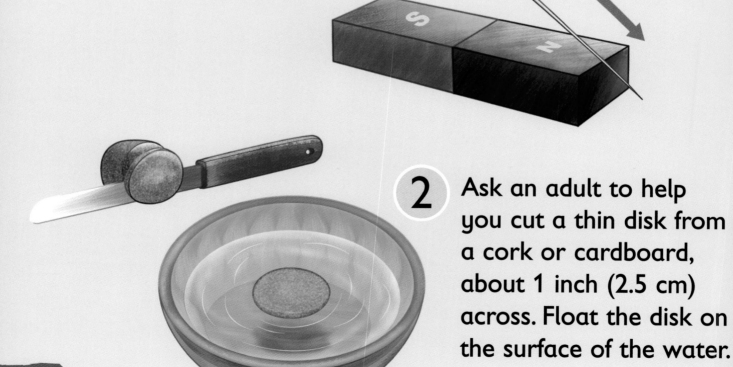

2 Ask an adult to help you cut a thin disk from a cork or cardboard, about 1 inch (2.5 cm) across. Float the disk on the surface of the water.

3 Carefully place your magnetized needle on top of the cork or cardboard. What happens?

What happened?

Stroking the needle magnetizes it and turns it into a compass needle. When the needle is left to float on the water, it slowly turns to point toward Earth's North Pole.

Using Magnets

Magnets are used in cell phones, loudspeakers, computer hard drives, magnetic catches on doors, and anything with an electric motor inside it.

Computer Magnets

Computer hard drives are disks covered with tiny metal particles. When you press a key on the computer keyboard, information is recorded on the disk by turning the tiny metal particles into magnets.

▶ *A computer reads a disk by changing the information held in the tiny magnets back into words and numbers.*

Making Sound

The sound from a television or radio comes out of loudspeakers. Inside each loudspeaker is a coil of copper wire inside a magnet. The coil vibrates when electricity passes through it. The coil is fixed to a large cone which also vibrates and makes the sounds we hear.

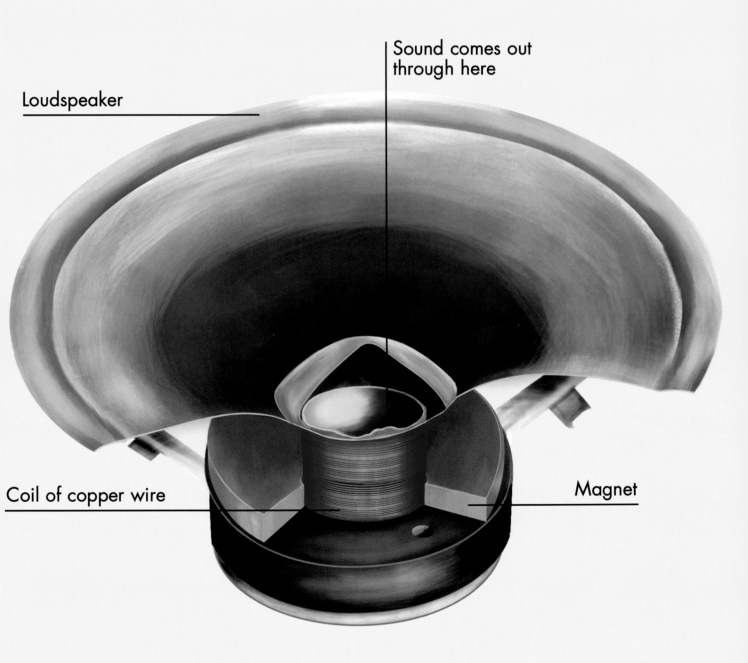

Sound comes out through here

Loudspeaker

Coil of copper wire

Magnet

▲ *This loudspeaker has been cut away to show the coil of gold-colored wire sitting inside the gray magnet.*

Magnetic Trains

The world's most advanced trains have no wheels. Powerful magnets help them float above the track. These trains are called **maglevs.**

Lifting Trains

This train floats along just above a rail. There is an electromagnet inside the train and the rail is a magnet, too. The two powerful magnets push each other away. Because of this, the train floats above the rail as it moves.

◀ *This maglev is used for scientific research on a test track in Japan.*

Green track magnet

Red train magnet

Let's Go!

Magnets not only support the weight of a maglev train, they make it move, too. The magnets in front of the train attract it and the magnets behind repel it. Because the train doesn't touch the track, it can go much faster than ordinary trains with wheels.

▼ *Magnets pull the train along the track. Many maglevs are built above ground level.*

Words to Remember

attract
To pull an object by an invisible force.

compass
An instrument that shows where north is. The compass needle is a tiny magnet which is attracted by the magnetic poles of the Earth.

core
The center of the Earth.

electric motor
A machine that uses magnets to change electricity into movement, usually by spinning a shaft, or rod.

electromagnet
A coil of wire, usually wound around an iron rod, that becomes magnetic when an electric current flows through the wire.

generator
A machine that uses magnets to produce electricity.

lines of force
Imaginary lines that join a magnet's north pole to its south pole.

loudspeaker
A device that uses a magnet to change an electric current into sound.

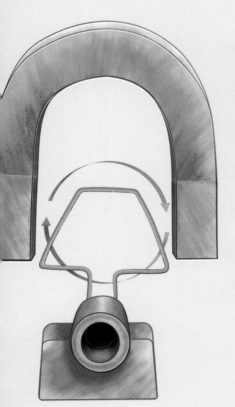

maglev
A maglev is a type of train that uses magnetic forces to float above its track. The word maglev is made from magnetic levitation, which means rising in the air due to magnetism.

magnet
An object that attracts the metals iron, cobalt, or nickel and most kinds of steel.

magnetic field
The area around a magnet where objects are affected by magnetic forces.

poles
The two parts of a magnet where magnetic force is strongest—the north pole and the south pole.

power plant
A place where electricity is made.

repel
To drive or force something away.

Index

Web Finder

For Kids:

http://www.coolmagnetman.com/magindex.htm

http://www.factmonster.com/ce6/sci/A0859426.html

For Teachers:

http://www.cln.org/themes/magnetism.html

http://atozteacherstuff.com/Themes/Magnets/

http://www.reachoutmichigan.org/funexperiments/quick/magnetfun.html